WHO MADE MY LUNCH?

FROM MILK TO CHEESE

BY BRIDGET HEOS · ILLUSTRATED BY STEPHANIE FIZER COLEMAN

AMICUS ILLUSTRATED and **AMICUS INK**
are published by Amicus
P.O. Box 1329, Mankato, MN 56002
www.amicuspublishing.us

**LIBRARY OF CONGRESS
CATALOGING-IN-PUBLICATION DATA**
Names: Heos, Bridget, author. | Coleman, Stephanie Fizer,
    illustrator. | Heos, Bridget. Who made my lunch?
Title: From milk to cheese / by Bridget Heos ; illustrated by
    Stephanie Fizer Coleman.
Description: Mankato, MN : Amicus, [2018] | Series: Who
    made my lunch?
Identifiers: LCCN 2016057203 (print) | LCCN 2017000526
    (ebook) | ISBN 9781681511191 (library binding) | ISBN
    9781681512099 (ebook) | ISBN 9781681521442 (pbk.)
Subjects: LCSH: Cheese—Juvenile literature. |
    Cheesemaking—Juvenile literature. | Dairy products—
    Juvenile literature.
Classification: LCC SF271 .H46 2018 (print) | LCC SF271
    (ebook) | DDC 637/.3—dc23
LC record available at https://lccn.loc.gov/2016057203

EDITOR: Rebecca Glaser
DESIGNER: Kathleen Petelinsek

Printed in China
HC 10 9 8 7 6 5 4 3 2 1
PB 10 9 8 7 6 5 4 3 2 1

ABOUT THE AUTHOR
Bridget Heos is the author of more than 80 books
for children. She lives in Kansas City with her
husband and four children. Her favorite cheese
is parmesan.

ABOUT THE ILLUSTRATOR
Stephanie Fizer Coleman is an illustrator, tea
drinker, and picky eater from West Virginia, where
she lives with her husband and two silly dogs. When
she's not drawing, she's getting her hands dirty in the
garden or making messes in the kitchen.

Cheddar cheese is tangy and delicious. In fact, it's the most popular cheese in the world! But what if you had to make it yourself? And also raise the cows that produce the milk?

Roll up your sleeves! You now work at a farmstead dairy.

At many dairy farms, milk is sent away to cheese factories.

But here, the cheese is produced right on the farm.

It takes 10 pounds (4.5 kg) of milk to make 1 pound (.45 kg) of cheese. So to make a lot of cheese, you need hundreds, or even thousands, of dairy cows.

All the cows need to be fed twice a day. Pour the feed mix into the troughs. And let the cows out to graze on grass in the pasture.

The cows are busy being milked, so you'll need to feed the calves. Want a vacation after all that work? Cows never take a day off, so you'll need a cow-sitter.

The cows will come inside when they're ready to be milked. A machine does the job. First it cleans the cows' udders. Then it suctions milk from them. The milk is stored in a refrigerated tank.

Different cheeses use different ingredients. The steps also vary slightly from cheese to cheese. Mozzarella, for instance, has to be stretched and pulled under warm water. But we are making cheddar. So let's get to work!

Time to make the cheese! The milk travels through underground tubes from the farm to the cheese-making factory. The first step is to kill any bad bacteria by pasteurizing, or heating, the milk.

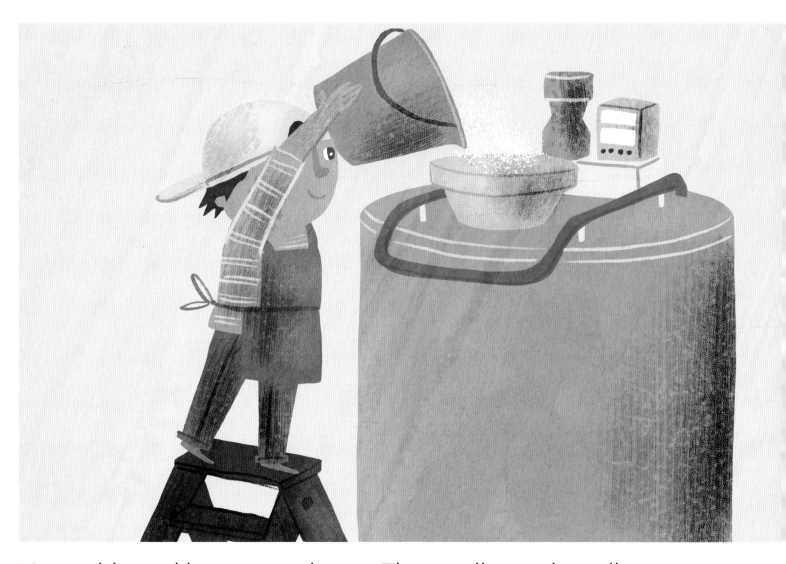

Now add good bacteria cultures. These will turn the milk into cheese and give it flavor. Then add a powder called rennet to help thicken the milk.

Stir all the ingredients together. Look, the milk is getting thicker. Use wire to cut through it. The solid pieces are called curds. The liquid that remains is whey. Drain the whey.

Next, shovel the curds together to form large hunks.

Slice, stack, and restack the hunks, allowing more of the whey to drain.

The hunks still contain too much moisture. Throw the hunks into the mill, which will chop them up.

Add salt. At this point, the cheese curds could be eaten as a yummy snack.

Ahem. But we still have work to do. Press the curds into metal forms. The cheese press will squeeze out even more whey. The forms will give the cheeses their shapes.

Finally, wrap the rounds of cheese in plastic or wax.
Store them in boxes in a refrigerated room, until
they are ready to be sold.

Thanks to the dairy farmers and the cheese makers,
you now have delicious cheddar cheese. Yes, please!

WHERE ARE DAIRY COWS RAISED?

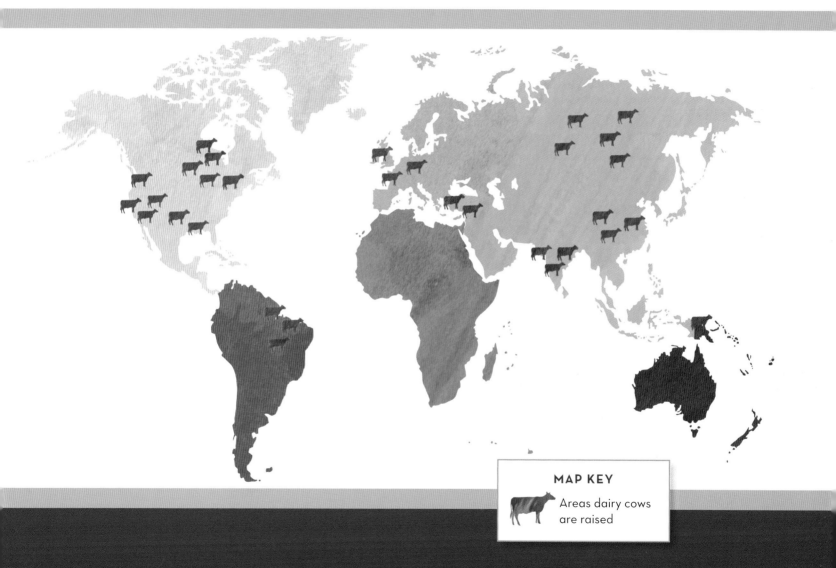

MAP KEY

Areas dairy cows
are raised

GLOSSARY

bacteria Microscopic, single-celled living things that can be either helpful or harmful.

cultures Good bacteria that are used to change milk into cheese.

curd The solid part of milk that is separated, often used to make cheese.

farmstead dairy A business that makes milk products using milk produced on the farm.

mill A machine that chops material into smaller pieces.

pasteurize To heat to a high temperature for the purpose of killing harmful bacteria.

whey The watery part of milk that separates from the solids when you make cheese.

WEBSITES

Discover Dairy
http://www.discoverdairy.com/
Watch a video and find other resources about milk production, including lesson plans.

Farms for City Kids: Making the Cheese
http://farmsforcitykids.org/about-our-cheese/making-the-cheese/
This farm in Vermont explains how they make their cheese.

My American Farm
http://www.myamericanfarm.org/
Games and educational resources from the American Farm Bureau help you learn where food comes from.

Every effort has been made to ensure that these websites are appropriate for children. However, because of the nature of the Internet, it is impossible to guarantee that these sites will remain active indefinitely or that their contents will not be altered.

READ MORE

Herrington, Lisa M. *Milk to Ice Cream.* New York: Children's Press, 2013.

Owings, Lisa. *From Goat to Cheese.* Minneapolis: Lerner, 2015.

Tuminelly, Nancy. *Let's Cook with Cheese!: Delicious and Fun Dishes Kids Can Make.* Minneapolis: ABDO Pub. Co., 2013.